ABOUT THE AUTHOR

Marie Segal was fascinated by the arts at an early age, beginning oil painting at age 10 and venturing into ceramics at 14. She worked with ceramic clay for years, until discovering polymer, an emerging medium that sparked a new rash of creativity. Marie sold handmade jewelry, gifts and home décor items, and later worked with a manufacturer, Polyform Products, to develop a new, colorful polymer clay called Premo! Sculpey. With this product, Marie helped elevate polymer clay to the status of a fine art medium. She now teaches internationally, authors how-to books and is featured in videos, magazines and on television. Marie and her husband, Howard, own and operate The Clay Factory, a polymer clay distribution and technical support company in Escondido, California. The couple has three grown daughters and lives in Escondido.

DEDICATION

This book is dedicated to my husband, who has worked side by side with me throughout these years, and has been my driving force, my ballast, manager, promoter, money man, and the all-time best husband and father. Also, to my parents, who gave me the chance to pursue my artistic goals, and to all the artists and friends who have always been so willing to listen and to share.

ACKNOWLEDGMENTS

I would like to thank Chuck and Denice Steinmann, owners of Polyform Products, for their vision and friendship. Also, thank you to my friend, syn holt, for teaching me all I needed to know about the computer/camera connection. Thank you to the great people at Banar Designs: Jeri, Barbara, Nancy and Steve.

T A B L E   O F

Textured Tile
Pot
11

Colorful
Necklace
and
Earrings
15

Antiqued
Drawer
Knobs
21

Terra-Cotta
Tile
13

Keeper of
Memories
18

East Meets
West
26

CONTENTS

Designer
Jewelry
29

Exotic Golden
Frame
33

Glowing Leaf
Votive
36

Mokume
Gane
Goblets
40

Amazing
Caned
Necklace
43

MARIE'S SUPPLY LIST

Clay

Polymer clay and polyclay are generic names for a synthetic modeling that can be baked in an ordinary oven. Crafters who have discovered this wonderful medium use it for jewelry making, doll making, greeting card embellishments, as well as many other crafting projects. There are many types of polymer clays on the market. Each one has its own qualities and properties. I would suggest that you experiment with various clays to discover the one you prefer.

For this book I have used Premo! Sculpey, a clay that my husband and I developed with Polyform Products. So of course I'm partial to this clay. It combines workability with strength and is easy to condition and work with, while being firm enough for creating all of the designing that I do with clay.

Polymer clay is sold in 2-ounce (56g) packages (sometimes called blocks), or 1 lb. (.45kg) bricks, in a wide variety of colors.

Cutting tools

I use a craft knife for detail cutting and other delicate work. For slicing and cutting straight lines I use a Sculpey Super Slicer or a tissue blade.

Pasta machine

My favorite tool is the pasta machine. It's worth every penny that you spend. The pasta machine is used to condition the clay and to make it into nice uniform sheets. The machines vary. The one I use is the Atlas by Marcato that goes from a #1 setting (thickest opening) to a #7, which is the thinnest. In my instructions, I'll tell you to roll your clay through either a thick, medium or thin setting. If your machine differs in the type of settings, you'll have to experiment to get the proper thickness of your clay.

Rollers

If you don't have a pasta machine, acrylic rollers work just fine for rolling out your clay and making uniform sheets. It just takes a bit longer. You can also use a tall, thin glass bottle or a smooth rolling pin to roll out clay.

Templates

These are thin acrylic sheets of die-cut designs. You use them to trace and then cut designs out of your clay. Polyform has a line of templates called Shapelets that offer a wide variety of shapes.

Push molds

With push molds you just push your clay into the mold and out pops a beautiful design that can be baked, decorated with paints or powders and then glued to a surface. There are many molds to choose from with a myriad of designs. The molds are used to create embellishments.

Texture plates

Texture plates are thin acrylic sheets with a design impressed on them. You use these to add all kinds of textures and designs to your clay by laying the plate on the clay and rolling through the pasta machine.

Cutters

These are similar to cookie cutters. You use them to cut out various shapes from a sheet of clay. Kemper cutters have plungers that make it easy to release the cut clay from the cutter. The cutters come in a variety of shapes and sizes. There are lots of other things that can be used, such as canape cutters and small cookie cutters. For cutting circles, I sometimes use the plastic canisters from 35mm film.

Needle tool

The needle tool is used for poking holes and for making impressions in the clay.

Rubber stamps

Stamps are wonderful for adding images and texture to polymer clay projects. They come in a giant assortment of designs. You can use any type of rubber stamp for impressing a image in the clay and adding texture and design.

Liquid polymer clay

This product has a variety of uses. I use Liquid Sculpey for affixing (gluing) baked or unbaked pieces of clay to others. This creates a better bond than glue does. It must be baked after it's applied in order to adhere. It can also be used as varnish to give a glossy, transparent finish. Or you can add oil paint to it and use it as a wash to add color to your project. When baking an object that has been painted or glazed with liquid polymer clay, bake at 275º (135º C) for 10 to 20 minutes.

Glues

My favorite glue is Crafter's Pick Ultimate Glue by Adhesive Products, Inc. I also use Superglue type gels for repairs and findings.

Baking tools

I use a regular cookie sheet lined with parchment paper or cardstock for baking most of my projects. If I want to add shine and smoothness to a project, I bake it on a sheet of glass. (See Amazing Caned Necklace, page 43.) This eliminates the buffing and polishing step.

Work surface

I mainly use a ceramic tile as a work surface or a flexible cutting board.

Finishes

For a lovely metallic finish, I use Pearl-Ex Powders by Jacquard. These are applied with cosmetic sponges. Other decorations for clay include gold leaf sheets, transfer foils, inks, glazes and paints.

Varnishes

Sculpey Glazes come in satin and gloss finishes. They are air-drying glazes for all baked clay products.

Additional supplies

Ruler
Pen and pencil
Paintbrush
Cosmetic sponges
Toothpicks
Craft sticks
Cookie sheet
Sponges and soft cloth
Spatula
Spray bottle

ABOUT POLYMER CLAY

If you haven't yet heard of polymer clay, or experimented with this remarkable, creative medium, it's definitely time that you did! Originally used by European doll and miniatures artists, this low-fire, synthetic clay is as versatile as can be, and works with many traditional crafter's tools to create wonderful decorative pieces.

Polymer can be stamped, molded, painted, sanded, cut, carved, drilled and texturized. You can mix it with a variety of things to enhance its capabilities. Flowers, herbs, glitter, crayon shavings, sand—these are just some of the possibilities. With add-ins, this incredible material is a perfect mimic. It can imitate the qualities of stone, ceramics, metal, even glass!

If you are new to polymer clay, don't worry—most beginners make leaps and bounds in a short period of time. Perhaps the most important thing about polymer is that it's great fun, whether you're "serious" or just playing around. Exploring the wonders of this medium, most people love the immediacy, as compared to ceramics, and the fact that it needs no painting because the color is built right in. Personally, I love having a piece of three-dimensional, pliable color to pick up and manipulate.

There's truly no limit to what you can do with polymer clay. This medium has kept my interest for 25 years and counting, and I'm someone with a somewhat short attention span! So, come, join me—let's play!

TECHNIQUES

Conditioning and rolling the clay:

All polymer clays need to be conditioned in order to redistribute the molecules and make it ready for use.

To condition clay using the pasta machine:

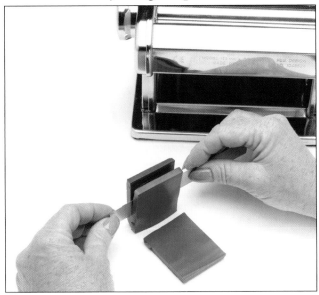

1. Cut the clay block into thirds.

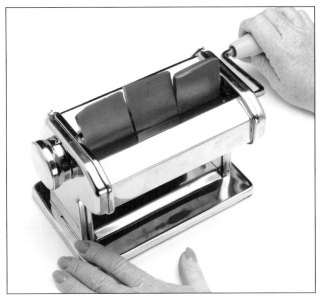

2. Place the three pieces side by side and roll through the pasta machine on the thickest setting. Cut another block into thirds and roll through the pasta machine. Put both of these sheets on top of each other and roll through the machine again on the thickest setting.

3. Fold in half and put the folded part into the pasta machine and roll through again. Keep repeating until you have a nice smooth sheet (usually 7 to 8 times).

4. Rolling the clay: After the clay has been conditioned it needs to be rolled out (just like cookie dough!). The best way to do this is to use the pasta machine. When instructions say to roll out on the thickest setting, it means the sheet should be rolled to about ⅛" (0.32cm).

To condition clay by hand:

If you don't have a pasta machine, cut off a section from the block of clay and roll between your palms. Fold the clay in half and roll again. Keep working this way until your clay is a nice, smooth consistency.

To roll clay by hand:

To roll clay into a sheet, you can use a brayer or acrylic roller. To make an even sheet, you can roll your clay between two craft sticks that act as guides. Flatten the clay into a pancake with your fingers and place between the two craft sticks. Then roll with the brayer or rolling pin to the thickness of the sticks, about ⅛" (0.32cm).

Making a Skinner shade: This is a method of creating a blended clay that transitions smoothly from one color to another, developed by clay artist Judith Skinner.

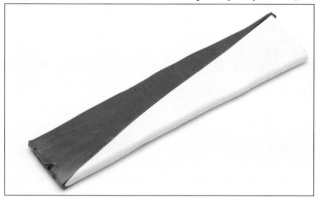

1. Start with triangles of clay, in this case two white and two green (you can use any combination of colors, e.g. red and blue or black and white). Stack the two green and two white triangles for double thickness of each triangle. The triangles will be 1" (2.5cm) in height. Make the length of the triangles the width of your pasta machine. Put the two triangles together to form a rectangle (see photo above).

2. Roll this through the pasta machine on the thickest setting. Bring out the sheet in front of you the way it comes out of your machine and fold in half lengthwise (see photo above).

Place the fold into the pasta machine and roll through again. Do this folding in half and putting through the machine 20 to 25 times until the colors blend from light to dark.

Making a Skinner sheet coil:

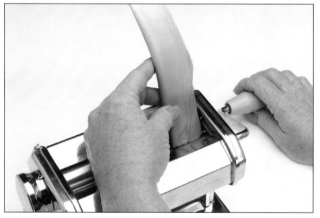

1. Fold the blended sheet in half and rotate it 90º to the right and place in the pasta machine lengthwise. Roll through on a much thinner setting. You will then have a long thin sheet.

Place the long sheet in front of you and trim the light colored edge off using your blade.

2. Roll this trimmed piece into a log to fit the end of the long thin sheet. This forms the center of the coil.

3. Roll up the sheet into a cane that goes from light in the middle to dark on the outside. This cane will then be reduced (see page 9) and incorporated into a design.

See examples of Skinner sheets on pages 37 and 44.

MORE TECHNIQUES

Making clay balls

Place clay between your palms. Apply light pressure, rotating in small circles.

Making logs

Squeeze kneaded clay roughly into a log shape. Roll back and forth between your palms to smooth and lengthen. Lay this on a work surface and roll back and forth lightly  with your fingers spread out. Keep it even as you roll.

Millefiore

This is a popular technique often used for jewelry. Millefiore gets its name from a similar technique in glass making. Canes of different shapes and thicknesses are combined into a single cane to build an image. After creating the cane, it is pulled or rolled into a longer shape (called reducing), which makes the image smaller. Slices are cut to display the design and are then baked. (For an example of a Millefiore project, see Amazing Caned Necklace, page 43.)

Reducing canes

This step is very critical when making millefiore projects. First build your cane, then "choke" the cane in the middle to form a waist, which will make the

 cane just slightly smaller. Rotate the cane and press it, working from the center to the top of the cane. Turn the cane over and work from the center to what used to be the bottom. Reduce the cane to half the width of the original before starting to reduce by rolling it on the table. This compacts the design inside the cane equally from all sides forcing the center out, which reduces any distortion in the design.

Cutting the cane

Some people say to let your cane sit and cool overnight before slicing it. But I usually can't wait to see the design. So in order to cut it right away, I pick it up and yank on both ends and then cut the cane in the middle. I also do what I call a rock and roll cut by rocking the blade up and down in a see-saw motion while cutting.

Transferring foils

There are many different types of foils available. I use foils that are made for decorating fabric such as tee-shirts. These are available in lots of interesting variegated designs and are much less expensive than using metallic leaf. To use the foil, lay out your clay in very thin sheets. Place the foil color-side-up on the clay leaving one edge over the clay, so that you can grab it later on.

With the sharp edge of your blade, scrape or drag it at a 45º angle across the foil-covered clay. Scrape several times from top to bottom and left to right. Pull the free edge up and away as fast as you can. The foil will be left  on the clay. For an example of a transfer foil project see Designer Jewelry (page 29).

Glazing and painting

Before you bake your clay project, you might want to paint or glaze it. There are several products available for this. I particularly like using Piñata Inks and I also use oil paints for certain projects. Acrylic paints work just fine. If you just want a nice finish on the project, there are several glazes available in either matte, satin or gloss finishes. To try out different paints or glazes, I like to bake a small piece of clay then paint it with the glaze or paint. I let it dry in the hot sun for 2 hours, bring it back into the house and let it cool. If the paint or glaze remains sticky, I don't use it.

When using Sculpey glazes, I like to put the glazed object in the oven at 200º (93ºC) for 10 minutes, take it out and let it cool.

Baking

Bake several pieces at once. When I have a complete cookie sheet filled, I preheat the oven and the sheet of pieces at 200º (93ºC) for 30 minutes. Then I bake the pieces according to the manufacturer's temperatures—usually this will be at 275º (135ºC) for 20 to 30 minutes. This way the pieces are baked or cured all the way through. Shut off the oven and let the pieces cool in the oven for about an hour before removing the sheet.

Inclusions (Mixing things in with clay)

A lot of things can be mixed in with your clay for special effects. I've used such things as flower petals, embossing powders, glitters, herbs, crayons, glass beads, sand, even dirt! It's interesting to mix flowers and herbs with translucent clay. Dry the flowers and herbs before you mix with the clay and they will retain their color. Instructions for adding inclusions are on page 27, step 4.

Safety

1. Be careful when using your oven, or when slicing or cutting with the sharp blades.

2. Wash your hands thoroughly after working with clay.

3. Wear latex gloves or barrier creams to protect hands.

4. The pasta machine and other tools that you use for polymer clay should never be used for food.

5. Bake clay in a well ventilated room. If the clay burns in the oven, don't breathe in the fumes.

6. Never use polymer clay pieces for drinking or eating.

7. Be careful that a child or pet doesn't swallow the clay.

GLOSSARY

Bone: creating a faux-ivory look from white and ecru clay.

Brayer: a rolling pin with a handle used for smoothing, flattening and rolling clay.

Cane: a technique where a design is constructed using long logs lengthwise, allowing for identical slices of the same design.

Condition: to mix and soften the clay into a workable state by kneading by hand or running through a pasta machine.

Cure: to bake the clay so that it sets permanently and is no longer soft or workable.

Findings: components used to make jewelry such as clasps, jump rings and pin backs.

Gold leaf: very thin sheets of metal in gold, bronze and silver or variegated.

Inclusion: substances that are mixed into clay such as glitter, herbs, flower petals and powders.

Log: a cylinder of clay.

Millefiore: canes constructed with a pattern running through the length, which can then be sliced and used for jewelry making or other embellishing.

Mokume Gane: a type of Japanese metal working. With clay, it involves stacking different colors and layers of clay (and sometimes gold leaf) and taking slices off of the stack, revealing interesting designs.

Needle tool: a pointed tool used for poking holes or adding designs to clay.

Pasta machine: usually used for making pasta, now it's an invaluable clay tool. The machine has two rollers that are turned by a handle. It's used for conditioning the clay, mixing colors and rolling out thin sheets.

Powders: mica powders used to create metallic and iridescent effects when applied to the clay.

Polymer clay: a synthetic modeling material that is cured in an ordinary oven.

Reduce: to make a cane smaller by squeezing, choking, rolling or pounding. The cane will end up with a smaller design pattern running through it.

Sheet: a thin flat piece of clay, usually made with a pasta machine or by rolling out with a brayer or rolling pin.

Skinner blend (shade): creating smooth gradations of color from triangular sheets of two different colors of clay, folding and running through the pasta machine several times. Developed by Judith Skinner.

Texture plates: thin acrylic sheets with different designs that can be pressed onto the clay to add texture.

Translucent clay: a clay that allows light to pass through it. The thinner the clay, the more translucent it will be.

TEXTURED TILE POT

Distinguish yourself with unique flower pots that are definitely not run of the mill. Accented with a handsome dark grout, this stamped, mosaic design is a fresh trend-setter that will certainly impress the neighbors. (It's likely to invite queries from many who may be unfamiliar with polymer clay!)

The clay is cut into many small squares for stamping. An eclectic mix of texturizing stamps creates an interesting combination as the pieces are glued around a plain pot. After baking, the grout is applied, then an antique finish of guilding paste is added, combining perfect, subtle colors to this artistic design.

Supplies:

4" (10cm) terra-cotta pot
2-ounce (56g) blocks of polymer clay: 1 each Cadmium Red and Raw Sienna (Premo! Sculpey)

Non-sanded grout, black
Olive Gold gilding paste (Rub 'N Buff)
Rubber stamps

⅝" (1.5cm) square cutter (Kemper)
Spray bottle with water
Pasta machine
Craft glue (Ultimate)

Prep: Mix the block of Raw Sienna with ¼ block of Cadmium Red. Condition the clay.

1. Roll the clay through the pasta machine on the thickest setting. Cut out tiles (69 were used for this project) using the square cutter.

2. Mist the stamps lightly with water, then press each tile onto the stamps of your choice. Use as many different stamps as you like to give variety and texture to your tile pieces. (I used the Stylus Tip Molding Mats from Color Box because of the variety of patterns.)

3. When all of the squares are stamped, glue them to the pot ⅛" (0.32cm) apart starting at the top rim. If the squares don't fit when you get all the way around, trim to fit the space. Continue gluing until the entire pot is covered.

Bake in the oven (see page 9). Let cool.

4. Wipe the pot with a damp sponge. Add grout to the pot (follow directions on the package). Scrape off any excess grout using a spatula. With an almost dry sponge, wipe away any grout that is on the tiles. Let dry overnight. Clean the last of the grout off the tiles with a dry towel.

5. Rub Olive Gold Rub 'N Buff over the surface of the pot. Wipe with a soft cloth to buff.

TERRA-COTTA TILE

Ceramic tile is beautiful, but the time and expense involved can make this medium difficult to pursue. With polymer clay, it's easy and less costly to create one-of-a-kind artistic tiles for display in a frame or easel. In fact, you could even make a few of your own decorative accent tiles for a wall remodeling project—imagine that!

Brass stencils help decorate these square polyclay cut-outs with raised designs. This garden-themed piece features a large iris surrounded by other charming, outdoor specimens. Artfully arranged on a piece of plain tile, the images are glaze-painted after baking, then baked again. Terra-cotta grout adds to this fabulous mosaic look.

Supplies:

- 4" x 4" (10cm x 10cm) ceramic tile
- 2-ounce (56g) blocks of polymer clay: 1 each Raw Sienna and Cadmium Red (Premo! Sculpey)
- Blue, Green, Brown, Gold, Black, Grey, White ink (Piñata)
- Small round paintbrush
- Paint mixing tray
- Sculpey Glaze, gloss
- Non-sanded grout, terra-cotta
- 2 brass stencils, iris (Heritage Handcrafts) and garden motif (Stamporium)
- Acrylic rod roller
- Tissue blade
- Toothpick
- Craft glue (Ultimate)
- Pasta machine

Prep: Condition the clay by mixing one block of Raw Sienna with ¼ block of Cadmium Red. Put clay through the pasta machine on thickest setting.

1. Place the iris stencil on the sheet of clay and roll over it using the acrylic roller. Roll until the clay is level with the stencil, then remove the stencil.

2. The clay will be stuck to the work surface, so slide the slicer under the clay to remove it from the table. Cut around the image to form a 2⅛" x 1¾" (5.4cm x 4.4cm) rectangle.

3. Spread glue on the back of this piece using a toothpick and place in the middle of the ceramic tile.

4. Lay the garden motif stencil on the clay and roll as in step 1. Repeat this step until you have enough images to fit the tile.

5. Cut and fit clay pieces to the tile allowing ⅛" (0.32cm) space between each tile for the grout. Trim pieces where necessary.

6. Apply glue to the back of each square and affix to the tile.

7. Bake in the oven (see page 9). Let cool.

8. Paint the images using the small round brush and your choice of colors.

9. Bake in the oven at 275º (135º C) for 30 minutes. Let cool.

10. Use a spatula to spread grout into the spaces between the tiles. Scrape off grout from the face of tile. With a damp sponge wipe off excess grout.

Let sit for 30 minutes, then repeat wiping with a damp sponge. Let dry overnight.

This playful jewelry is great fun to wear and a joy to create, especially if you love to paint as well as work with clay. The terra-cotta-colored set has a wonderful arts 'n crafts feel, yet the beads are so perfect, it's hard to believe you made them yourself!

Several cutters are used to shape and imprint these polymer beads with raised images— whimsical flowers, hearts, stars, and the like. A mix of Liquid Sculpey and Piñata inks followed by gloss leaves gleaming areas that look like three-dimensional, set-in charms. Seed and bugle beads add to the beauty of these multi-colored pieces—a great accessory set for spring and summer.

COLORFUL NECKLACE AND EARRINGS

Supplies:

2-ounce (56g) blocks of polymer clay: 1 each Cadmium Red and Raw Sienna (Premo! Sculpey)
Liquid polymer clay (Sculpey)
White, Red, Yellow, Green, Blue and Purple ink (Piñata)
Sculpey Glaze, gloss

Paint mixing tray
Small round paintbrush
Seed beads, assorted colors
¼" (6mm) black bugle beads
Bead cord (Stretch Magic)
Cutters: ¾" (2cm) oval, ⅜" (0.95cm) oval, round, star, heart, teardrop and flower (Kemper)
Needle tool

Slide cutters
2 each 2" (5cm) gold head pins
2 French wire earring findings
Round nose pliers
Craft glue (Ultimate)
Pasta machine

Prep: To condition the clay, mix a block of Raw Sienna with ¼ block of Cadmium Red. Roll through the pasta machine on the thickest setting.

1. Cut out 76 ovals with the ¾" (2cm) oval cutter.

2. Place the needle tool across the longest part of one oval.

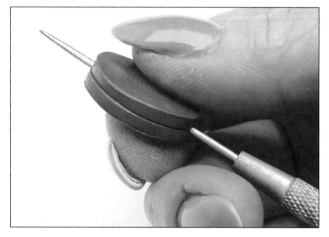

3. Place another oval on top and press together.

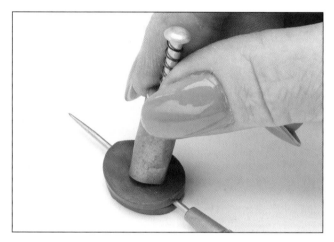

4. Make an imprint on both sides of the bead using the cutter.

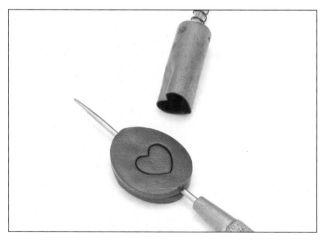

5. Make imprints in the other beads using an assortment of the cutters as desired.

6. Remove the needle tool, then bake the beads (see page 9).

7. Paint all the beads on one side using the colors of your choice. Bake at 275º (135ºC) for 20 minutes. Shut off the oven and let cool. Paint the other side of the beads and bake again.

8. Paint each side of the beads with Sculpey Glaze, drying after painting each side. Let dry.

Bake at 200º (93ºC) for 15 minutes. Let cool

9. String bugle beads and seed beads between the terra-cotta beads as shown on page 15. Tie the ends of the cord together with several square knots. Put a dab of glue on the knot and pull the knot into a terra-cotta bead to hide the knot.

10. To make the earrings: String beads on the head pins as follows: bugle bead, seed bead, terra-cotta bead, seed bead, bugle bead. Attach to earring findings.

KEEPER OF MEMORIES

Create this photo album to hold all your treasured memories. It's easily made by merely covering a purchased album with coordinating handmade papers, then adding embellishments of molded and colored polymer clay. Petite flowers, gold brushed tassels, and an Asian-inspired fan are framed within a bamboo enclosure.

As an alternative, use these same instructions to cover a journal—the perfect place to take notes at a meeting or jot down all your goals and dreams.

Supplies:

Photo album, 4" x 6" (10cm x 15cm)
Paper (Washi, mulberry or other soft fibrous paper)
2-ounce (56g) blocks of polymer clay: 2 Ecru, 1 each Ultramarine Blue, Green, Cadmium Red and Black (Premo! Sculpey)

Sheet of bone (see page 26)
Silver, Pearl and Gold powder (Pearl-Ex)
Texture plates: Asian flowers and vine
Asian motif templates (Sculpey Shapelets)
Push mold, Asian motif (Polyform)

Stamp, apple blossom (Polyform)
Midnight Blue stamp ink pad (Inkredibles)
Plastic knife and craft knife
Spray bottle with water
Cosmetic wedge
Craft glue (Ultimate)
Pasta machine

Prep: Mix ¼ block Green with ½ block Ecru for bamboo. Mix ¼ block Ultramarine Blue with ¼ block Ecru for background. Mix ¼ block Cadmium Red with ½ block Ecru for flowers. Condition the clay.

1. Roll background clay mix through the pasta machine on the thickest setting.

2. Cut the flowers and vine texture plate to 5½" x 8½" (14cm x 21.5cm). Mist the texture plate with water and place against the background clay, then roll through the pasta machine on the thickest setting. Release clay from texture sheet and cut to 3½" x 5½ (9cm x 21.5cm).

3. Dust the sheet with Pearl powder using a cosmetic wedge.

4. Mist the Asian mold. Press half of the bamboo clay mix into the bamboo mold. Make four bamboo pieces. Gently stretch two of the bamboo pieces to fit the long edge of the blue textured sheet. Glue to each side of the sheet with liquid polymer clay. Then glue the short bamboo pieces to the top and bottom, trimming to fit.

5. Mold 4 tassels using the Ultramarine + Ecru mix. Glue a tassel in each corner (as pictured) using liquid polymer clay.

6. Cut a fan shape from the bone sheet using the fan template.

7. Stamp this with the apple blossom stamp and Blue ink. Let dry.

8. Roll the red flower clay mix through the pasta machine on the thickest setting. Mist the flowers and vine texture plate and roll the clay and plate through the machine on the thickest setting.

Peel the clay away from the sheet. Using a craft knife, cut out two single flowers from the textured clay. Glue a flower to each side of the bamboo (refer to photo) using liquid polymer clay.

9. Glue the bone fan shape in the center of the blue sheet using liquid polymer clay.

10. Roll Black clay through the thickest setting on the pasta machine and mist the fan side of the texture plate. Roll the clay and texture plate through the pasta machine on the thickest setting. Cut out the fan shape and dust with Silver powder. Glue the fan to the bone piece using liquid polymer clay.

11. Bake the completed clay piece in the oven (see page 9). Set aside to cool.

12. Cover the photo album with the decorative paper and glue the clay piece to the front of the album using craft glue.

ANTIQUED DRAWER KNOBS

What satisfaction—transforming the look of a plain old dresser with the addition of beautiful antiqued-brass drawer knobs! No one would ever suspect, but these "metal" knobs are the creative result of a morning's fun with polymer clay.

The project starts with a package of black clay cut into circles for molding around ceramic or wooden knobs. Twisted coil trim and other details are created by hand and with a needle tool, then gold pigment powder and glaze create the gleaming finish, virtually indistinguishable from real metal. There's reason to be proud when you've spruced up a bedroom and had such a great time in the process!

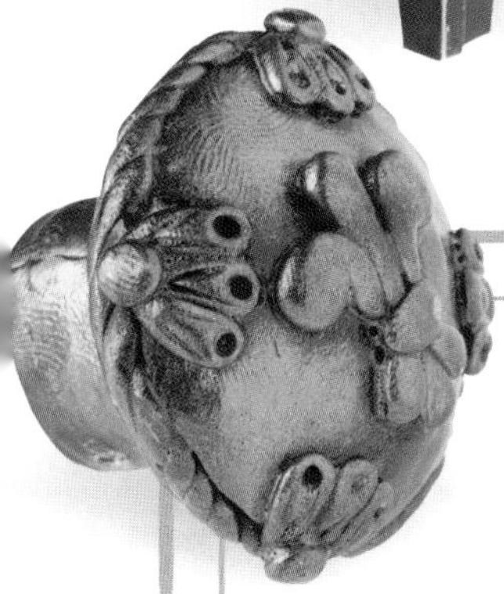

Supplies

4 ceramic knobs
2-ounce (56g) block of polymer
   clay: Black (Premo! Sculpey)
Aztec Gold powder (Pearl-Ex)
Sculpey Glaze, gloss

Two circle templates
Craft knife
2" (5cm) round cutter (Kemper)
Needle tool
Ballpoint pen
Pasta machine

Prep: Condition the clay. Put the clay through the pasta machine on the thickest setting.

1. Cut out two large circles (per knob) using the 2" (5cm) round cutter (adjust size to fit your particular knob). Cut the center from one large circle to fit the shaft of your knob.

2. Press one circle firmly to the top of the knob.

3. Place the knob through the opening of the second circle and press to the underside of the knob.

4. Pinch the two circles together on the edge of the knob, leaving a ⅛" (0.32cm) channel between the two pieces.

5. Cut a strip long enough to go around the shaft of the knob. Wrap it around the shaft, butting the edges together. Press the clay to the knob and trim excess.

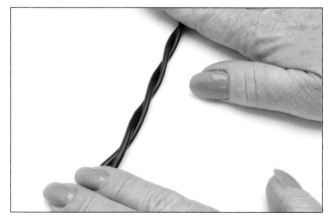

6. To make the rope trim: Roll out a ⅛" (0.32cm) log that is 10" (25.4cm) long. Fold in half, pull and twist making as even as possible.

7. Press the rope around the edge of the knob, placing it into the channel. Butt the ends and trim.

8. For knob embellishments: Roll black clay through the pasta machine on the thickest setting. Form 29 tiny balls of black clay. Roll into tear drop shapes as pictured in the diagram and apply to the knob as pictured. Affix the four remaining tiny balls to the ends of the teardrop shapes (see diagram).

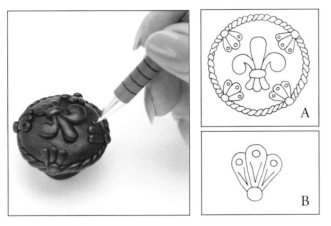

9. Create the center decoration with more balls of black polymer clay. Poke decorative holes in the end of the teardrop shapes (see diagram) using a ballpoint pen (A).

Use a needle tool to make indentations on the tear drop shapes as in diagram (B).

10. Dust the complete knob with Aztec Gold powder using a cosmetic wedge. Repeat steps for three remaining knobs.

Bake in the oven (page 9) and let cool. Paint with Sculpey Glaze and let dry. Bake again at 200º (93ºC) for 10 minutes. Add knobs to your favorite piece of furniture.

Hint:

When I am working with Pearl-Ex powders, I spread some out on a piece of paper and pick it up by rubbing the sponge in the powder. In this way I get an even distribution of the powder instead of clumps.

EAST MEETS WEST

Add drama to your jewelry collection with this lovely Asian inspired brooch and earring set. Incorporating the use of coins, stones, embossing powders, inks, molds and wire, this set is surprisingly easy to create. The tasseled embellishments are molded clay, baked, then painted and finished with a golden glow. Translucent stones are attached to the coins with artistically wrapped golden wires. The base of each piece is a jade-like stone created of clay. Once you've made this set of jewelry and learned the techniques, you're ready to go on to other unique and interesting projects.

EAST MEETS WEST

Supplies

2-ounce (56g) blocks of polymer clay: 1 each Black, White, Ecru and Translucent (Premo! Sculpey)
Liquid polymer clay (Sculpey)
Sculpey Glaze, gloss
Cyanoacrylate glue (Loc-tite or Superglue)

Embossing powder, verdigris
Aztec Gold powder (Pearl-Ex)
Black ink stamp pad (Inkredibles)
Rubber stamp (ERA Graphics)
Push mold, Asian motif (Polyform)

3 Chinese coins
3 crystal chunk beads
26-gauge wire, brass
2 each 10mm earring backs
2 earring clutches
Pin back
Tissue blade
Pasta machine
Round cutter (slightly larger than coins)
Wire cutters
Craft knife

To make the bone sheet: (this is a technique that I use to imitate striations in real bone or ivory)

Prep: Mix ⅓ block of Ecru clay with ⅓ block of White. Condition the Translucent and Black clay.

Roll the solid Ecru (not mixed with White) through the pasta machine on the thickest setting. Cut a sheet 4" x 2" (10cm x 5cm). Then do the same thing with the White and the Translucent clay.

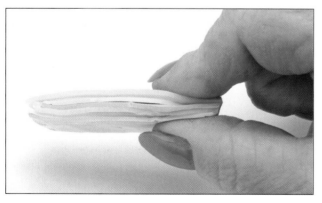

1. Stack the sheets in this order: Ecru, Ecru/White mix, White, and Translucent. Cut in half lengthwise.

Compress these two stacks together (make sure the same colors are not touching). Flatten and stretch out to 4" x 2" (10cm x 5cm) and cut in half again to 2" x 2" (5cm x 5cm).

Repeat these steps four more times.

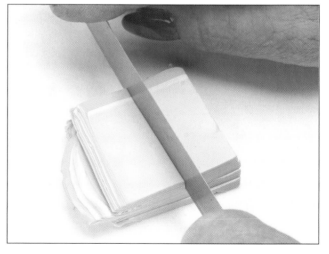

2. Cut this stack in half. Stack one on top of the other, but do not reduce and stretch.

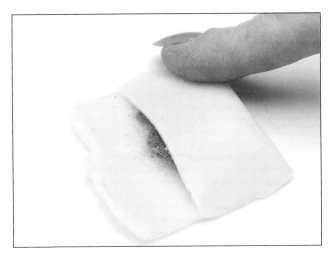

3. Slice off a ⅛" (0.32cm) sheet from the stack and put it through the pasta machine on the thickest setting with the lines going vertically.

Turn the sheet a quarter turn and put through the pasta machine horizontally on the next setting.

Put it through again on the next setting and repeat. Set aside the bone sheet you've just created.

To make the green jade clay: Condition ¼ block of the Translucent clay and roll it through the pasta machine on a medium setting.

4. Spread ½ teaspoon of verdigris embossing powder on the the center of the Translucent sheet.

Fold the sheet in thirds by folding the right third over the center and pressing the top and the bottom closed (as pictured).

Fold the left third over the center and press closed. Flatten with thumb and forefinger with the embossing powder inside. Fold in half and roll through the pasta machine on the thickest setting.

Fold in half again and roll through the pasta machine until the powder is evenly dispersed on the sheet.

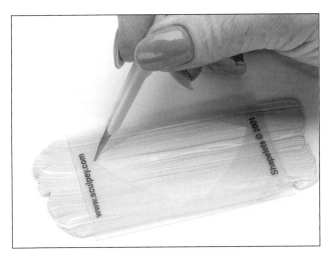

5. Roll out this sheet in the pasta machine on a medium setting. Cut three circles ⅛" (0.32cm) larger than the coins (two for earrings, one for the brooch).

6. Roll the slice of bone sheet you created previously through the pasta machine on a medium setting.

For the brooch, cut out a fan-shaped piece using the fan template.

Tip: There are many items around your house that would make good cutters for your clay projects. Look for such things as cookie cookers, small jars, film canisters, drinking glasses, coins, lipstick lids, donut cutter and jar tops.

7. Ink the stamp with black ink and press the fan bone piece lightly on the stamp. Allow to dry (about 6 hours).

Roll remainder of the jade sheet through the pasta machine on a medium setting.

8. Use the bone fan piece as a pattern and place it on the jade green piece. Cut ⅛" (0.32cm) larger all the way around.

Roll Black clay through the pasta machine on a medium setting. Place the jade fan piece on top of the black piece and cut ⅛" (0.32cm) larger all around.

9. Use liquid polymer clay to affix all the pieces, layering as shown above for the brooch.

10. Make two bamboo leaves and three tassels by pressing Black clay into the molds. Trim excess. Dust them with Aztec Gold powder. Affix the pieces to the brooch and earrings (as pictured on page 26) using liquid polymer clay.

11. Poke two holes in the center of the three coins using a toothpick, then bake all pieces in the oven (see page 9). Let cool.

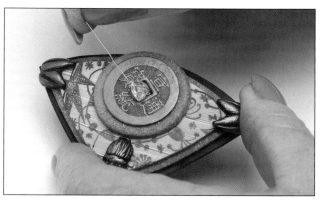

12. Thread wire through crystal and twist on back to secure. Going from front to back, thread ends of the wire through the holes in the coin. Bring the wire back through the front and wrap around the crystal two or three times. Twist the wire in back and trim.

Paint all tassels and leaves with Sculpey Glaze, then bake in a 200º (93ºC) oven. Let cool.

Glue pin back and earring findings.

DESIGNER JEWELRY

This beautiful necklace and earring set is an example of the amazing imitative qualities of polymer clay. With the enhancement of metallic foils and gloss, these formed clay pieces are very similar to shiny, multi-colored dichroic glass. The intense colors and texture add an exotic feel to these accessories, which will definitely make an artistic statement about the wearer.

The tools used here include shaping templates, stamping materials, variegated gold leafing and a texture plate. The pendant and earrings are three layers thick, including bold black, gold-leafed and foil-colored pieces. Make this set, then experiment with more and add "jewelry designer" to your repertoire!

Supplies:

2-ounce (56g) block of polymer clay: 1 Black (Premo! Sculpey)
Liquid polymer clay (Sculpey)
Variegated black or gold leaf (Old World Art)
Foil (Jones Tones)
Texture plate, African motifs (Shade Tex)

Classic motifs template (Sculpey Shapelets)
Triangle motifs template (Sculpey Shapelets)
Stamp (ERA graphics)
Black ink stamp pad (Inkredibles)
2 gold French wires
2 each 10mm jump rings

Flat head jewelry pliers
Round nose jewelry pliers
Tissue blade
Rubber cording, 18" - 30" (76cm)
Bamboo skewer
Craft glue (Ultimate)

Prep: Condition the clay. Roll it through the pasta machine on the thickest setting. The sheet should be about 2" x 3" (5cm x 8cm).

1. Lay the foil sheet on top of the clay and rub the surface with your finger. Leave a tab of the foil extending slightly at the top so that it will lift off easily (see transferring foils, page 9).

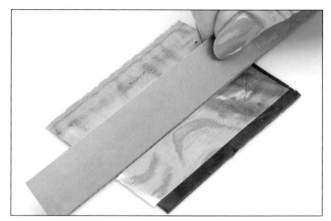

2. Rub the sharp edge of the slicing blade at a 45° angle over the the clay three to four times in each direction until the foil transfers to the clay.

3. Remove the film from the foil rapidly. (Touching the foil too much will dull it.)

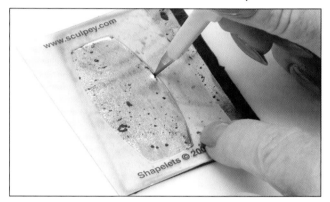

4. Place the Classic Shapelet template over the foil and cut out the shape using a craft knife. For earrings, cut two small triangles using the Triangle Shapelet or create your own shape.

5. Ink the stamp with the black stamp pad and press the rectangular piece and earring pieces onto the stamp. Allow to dry overnight.

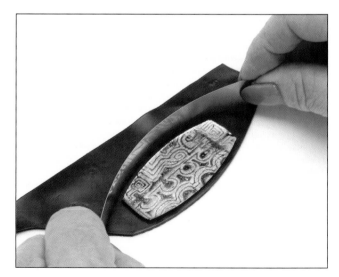

6. Lay the rectangular foil piece and earring pieces on a sheet of black clay. Using this piece as a guide, cut the black clay ⅛" (0.32cm) larger using the slicer blade (as pictured above).

7. Lay a piece of gold leaf on a sheet of black clay. Roll through the pasta machine on the thickest setting. Cut around as you did in step 6 (see photo).

To secure the piece while cutting, place a dab of liquid polymer clay on the back of the black pieces and place on the top of the gold leaf pieces.

8. Using a toothpick, poke holes in the top portion of the earrings going through all three layers.

9. To make tube beads: Roll a ¾" x 4" (2cm x 10cm) sheet of black clay around the bamboo skewer. Close the seam by smoothing with fingers. Roll on the table (not hard or fast). Loosen the clay from the skewer by giving it a few twists. Roll on the table again to smooth.

10. Cut one 1½" (4cm) section (not cutting through skewer) using the slicer blade. Slide bead off the skewer. Set aside.

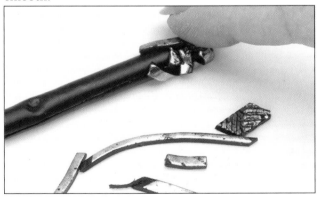

11. With the gold leaf and foiled sheet left over from steps 4 and 7, cut several small strips approximately ⅛" x ½" (0.32cm x 1cm) varying the sizes slightly. Add these strips randomly to the tube. Roll this tube on the table gently to adhere the foil and gold leaf strips. Cut the tube into ½" (1cm) sections.

12. For round beads: Make six ½" (1cm) balls and add the strips of foil randomly to each bead. Roll the beads gently between your palms to adhere the foil.

Drill a hole in each bead using the bamboo skewer.

Bake the pendant piece, earrings and beads in the oven (see page 9). Let cool.

13. Glue the 1½" (4cm) bead made in step 10 to the back of the pendant piece using liquid polymer clay and bake this piece again for the full time. Let cool.

Apply Sculpey Glaze to the foil and leafed sections of the jewelry. Bake in the oven at 200° (93°C) for 10 minutes and let cool completely.

Attach earring findings.

Glue cord into one end of the pendant tube. String beads as pictured on page 29. Glue the other end of the cord to the opposite end of the tube. Allow glue to dry for two days.

Hint:

After you're finished with your projects, don't throw away those scraps. Keep the scraps in plastic bags. I usually separate the scraps by color and technique, then when I'm ready to make beads I know just where to find the scraps that I need. They can be used to make beautiful jewelry—and most of the work is already done! See opposite for bead instructions and ideas.

MAKING BEADS FROM SCRAPS

To make scrap beads:

1. Gather a few small scraps together and wad them up into a loose ball so that you can still see the separate pieces. Roll gently between your palms to smooth.

2. Push a needle tool through the bead, carefully rotating as you push. Then push it back through the opposite side of the hole to neaten it.

3. Bake several beads at a time.

4. To antique bone beads: When cool, brush with Burnt Umber acrylic paint and a stiff brush. Work the paint into the cracks. Wipe off excess.

5. To make tube beads see page 31. Tube beads can also be wrapped in a sheet of scrap clay, such as bone or foil.

6. Experiment making different shapes and sizes with your scraps.

EXOTIC GOLDEN FRAME

This frame is every bit as beautiful as similar, more expensive counterparts. Allowing you to "play" with a single color of polymer clay and a variety of tools, this project is an artisan's dream. Sheets of gold leaf help create the gleaming surface while the texture plate adds design and fine detail.

Supplies:

Wooden picture
frame
2-ounce (56g) blocks
of polymer clay: 3
Black (Premo!
Sculpey)

Variegated gold leaf (Old
World Art)
Interference Red,
Interference Green and
Bronze powders (Pearl-
Ex)
Sculpey Glaze, gloss

Flexible push mold, African motifs
(Polyform)
African texture plate (Scratch Art)
Craft glue (Ultimate)
Tissue blade
Spray bottle with water
Cosmetic sponge
Toothpick
Pasta machine

Prep: Condition the clay. Roll it out on the pasta machine on a medium setting.

1. Place the Black clay on the sheet of variegated leaf while it is still in the "book." The leaf will adhere to the clay. Cut this sheet in half. Also cut the texture plate in half. Each piece should be 5½" x 8½" (14cm x 21.5cm).

2. Place the clay sheet, the foil sheet and the texture plate together into the pasta machine and roll through on a medium setting.

3. Glue the textured clay, one quarter at a time to the frame, smoothing down securely. Trim away the center part. Fold over the edge of frame, press and trim. Continue gluing the pieces to the other 3 sections of the frame. Slightly overlap the clay on the corners and trim away any excess. Butt the edges to match.

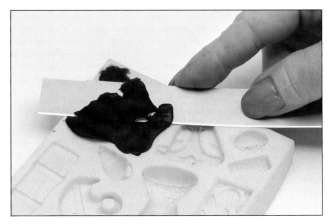

4. To mold the decorative corner squares, mist the mold with water. Roll Black clay into two 1" (1.2cm) balls and press them one at a time into the mold. Press and hold the clay with your fingers (the clay will try to come away from the wet mold). Trim away any excess using a blade. Remove pieces from the mold and dust with colored powders using a cosmetic sponge. Glue the squares to the top left and bottom right corners of the frame.

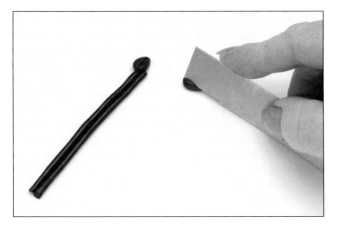

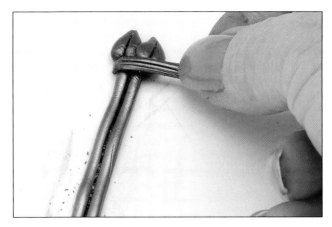

5. To make the rod embellishments, roll out four coils ⅛" (0.32cm) in diameter and 3" (7.62cm) long. Place two each of the coils together. Make four ¼" (0.64cm) balls of clay and roll into teardrops and flatten with fingers. With the back of the slicer, press down to make an impression in the teardrops (do not cut all the way through). Place one teardrop at the end of each coil.

6. Dust the rods with Bronze powder. Then dust the tops with Interference Red powder. Roll out a sheet of Black clay in the pasta machine on a medium setting. Cut two strips that are ⅛"(0.32cm) high and 1" (2.5cm) long. Score three stripes on each strip using the dull side of the slicer, then dust with Bronze powder. Lay the strip as pictured above and trim excess.

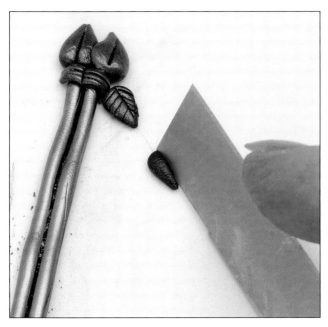

7. For the leaves: Make four ⅛" (0.32cm) balls and roll into an elongated teardrop. Flatten with finger. Score down the center, then score little marks from the top to bottom of the leaf, pointing down. Dust with Interference Green powder. Glue the two leaves to the top of each bronze rod (see photo).

8. Glue each decorated rod on the frame (refer to photo above).

Bake for 30 minutes at 275º (135ºC). Turn off the oven and let cool. Paint with Sculpey Glaze and let dry. Bake again at 200º (93ºC) for 15 minutes and again, let cool.

GLOWING LEAF VOTIVE

Using an ancient glass-art technique called Millefiore, you can create this gorgeous, glowing candleholder. Whether presented as a gift or displayed at home, this piece is definitely most impressive! People will be amazed that you made it yourself, but even as they exclaim, "I could never do that," you'll know the intricate appearance is a bit deceiving.

Supplies:
3" (7.62cm) glass vase
Pasta machine
Tissue blade
Toothpick

2-ounce (56g) blocks of polymer clay:
3 Translucent, 2 each Cobalt Blue,
Ultramarine Blue, Purple, Violet
(Premo! Sculpey)

Prep: Condition all clay.

Make Skinner shade sheets of each of the four colors of clay listed above. Each color will be made with the translucent clay. (See page 8 for instructions.)

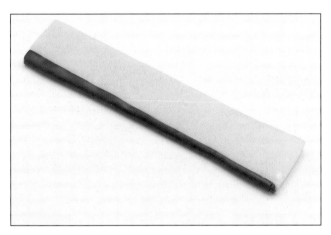

1. Make coils (see page 8) with each of the four sheets of Skinner blends. But use only ¼" (0.64cm) Purple triangle for the Purple /Translucent sheet.

2. Starting with your first colored coil, cut it into fourths. Repeat all of the steps (2 to 12) for each color of clay.

3. Roll additional Purple clay through the pasta machine on a thin setting.

4. Lay the end piece of the coiled log that you cut off in step 2 onto the flat sheet of purple to use as a cutting pattern. Cut three pieces this size. Set aside the unused sheet of Purple.

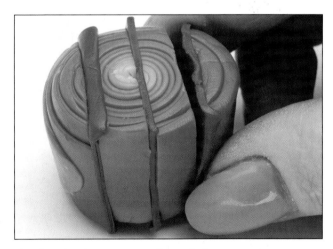

5. Slip the three pieces of Purple between the cut sections of the coiled log. Press these sandwiched pieces back together.

4. With the blade, cut across this log diagonally.

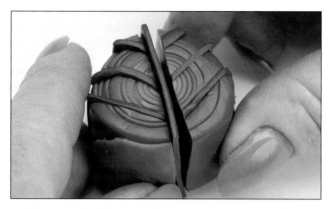

5. Turn one half upside down and put the two halves together as pictured so that the leaf veins are formed. Place one half on the retained Purple sheet and cut a piece to the length of the half. Place the piece between the halves. Press together.

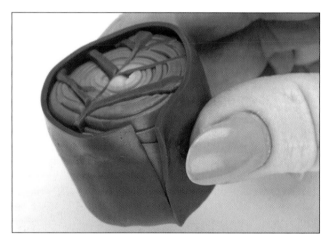

6. Place the log on the purple sheet and wrap the sheet around the log. Trim, then butt the cut edges together and press together until smooth.

7. To reduce the log: Place thumb and forefinger around the log and start pressing and rotating, working up and down to make the log smaller and compact. Reduce the log to half its original width.

8. Once you have reduced the log, roll it on the table starting in the center then move toward the ends as you roll. Reduce to approximately ⅝" (1.5cm) in diameter.

9. Cut off the ends with your blade.

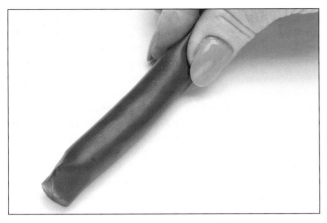

10. Pinch both ends of the log where the top of the leaf will be. Twist the log so that the back pinch and the front pinch line up. This will retain the leaf design if it has moved when you rolled it. Pinch down the center of the log.

11. Make a mark with the toothpick at each vein line on each side. Draw lines down the outside of the log with the toothpick, making indentations where the ends of each vein line are.

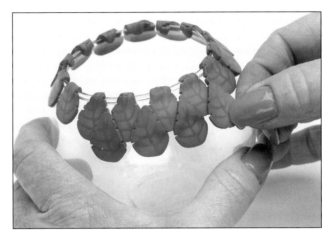

12. Slice off ¹⁄₁₆" (0.16cm) sections of the cane.
Repeat all of the steps with the other three colors of clay so that you'll have four different leaf colors.

13. Starting at the top of the votive, apply lightest color of leaves pointing up and slightly overlapping at the bottom. Gently press the leaves to the glass. Press the next row slightly overlapping the row above it. Continue adding leaves, three rows each of the four colors.

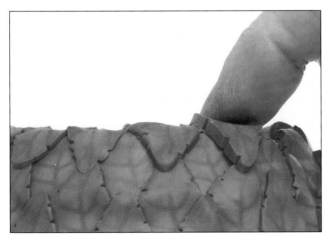

14. Add the row at the top of the votive, placing the leaves on the inside of the glass and then folding them over and down to the outside, all around.

15. Bake in the oven (see page 9). Shut off the oven and let cool. When finished, add a votive candle and admire your glowing vase.

MOKUME GANE GOBLETS

Not just any wine glasses will do for a very special toast. This pair is stunning—the stems seemingly cut from a beautiful slab of marbleized stone. Of course, it's polymer clay that creates this dramatic look, with the help of a Japanese metal-work technique called Mokume Gane.

The Asian method of combining sheets of colored metal is somewhat complicated, but with polyclay, the process is easy and virtually mistake-proof. In a series of steps, the clay sheets are stacked, compressed, cut and distressed until the colors and gold leafing merge into gorgeous, metallic swirls. The glass stems are covered with this clay design, along with black trim, then baked to glorious perfection!

Supplies:

Goblets
2-ounce (56g) blocks of polymer clay: 1 each Black, Gold, Translucent, White, Burnt Umber and Ecru (Premo! Sculpey)

Variegated gold leaf
Tissue blade
Small paintbrush
Pasta maker

Prep: Condition the clay. Roll each of the colors of clay through the pasta machine on a medium setting.

1. Cut one rectangle of each color 5" x 2" (12cm x 5cm) and two rectangles of Translucent clay to the same size. Place one sheet of Translucent clay on top of the variegated gold leaf. Pull up on the clay and the leaf will adhere to it. The other sheet of translucent clay will be used plain.

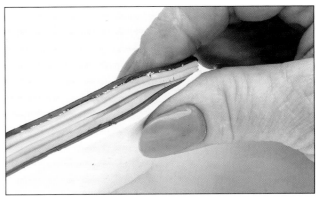

2. Stack the sheets as follows: White, Black, Burnt Umber, Translucent, Gold, Ecru, Translucent/ variegated gold leaf sheet. Cut the stack in half so that you have two pieces 2½" x 2" (6cm x 5cm). Stack one on top of the other and pinch the stack to compress and flatten to ½" (1cm) thick. Cut the stack in half again and repeat the pinching and flattening step.

3. Poke holes over the entire sheet using the handle end of the paintbrush. Cut the stack in half. Pinch and flatten to ½" (1cm).

4. Cut in half and place one on top of the other. Pinch this stack without flattening. Cut in half and stack again.

5. Use the slicer to sliver off thin slices from the stack.

6. Roll out a sheet of Black clay the width of your pasta machine by 4" (10cm). Place the slivered pieces on the black sheet covering it entirely. Do not overlap too much or make it too thick. Roll this sheet through the pasta machine at the thickest setting. Turn the sheet a quarter turn and run it through again at the next setting. Do this again on the next setting.

7. Cut the sheet the height of the stem x 4" (10cm). Wrap around the stem once and press tightly, then trim, butting edges together.

8. For coils: Roll out a coil of Black clay ⅜" (0.95cm) in diameter and as long as the black sheet. Lay the coil on the edge of the black sheet and roll it around the coil. Butt edges together, press and trim. Roll on the table and reduce the coil to ¼" (0.64cm) diameter.

9. Cut the ends of the coil at an angle and wrap around the base of the goblet. Butt ends together, press and trim. Make two more coils and wrap around two places at the top of the goblet stem as pictured on page 40.

10. Roll out six ⅛" (0.32 cm) diameter black coils and wrap around the stem above and below the larger coils. Press and trim the ends.

Bake in the oven (see page 9). Allow to cool.

Hint:
These goblets could also be used as candleholders for a festive dinner party. Just drop a bit of melted wax in the base of each and add coordinating taper candles.

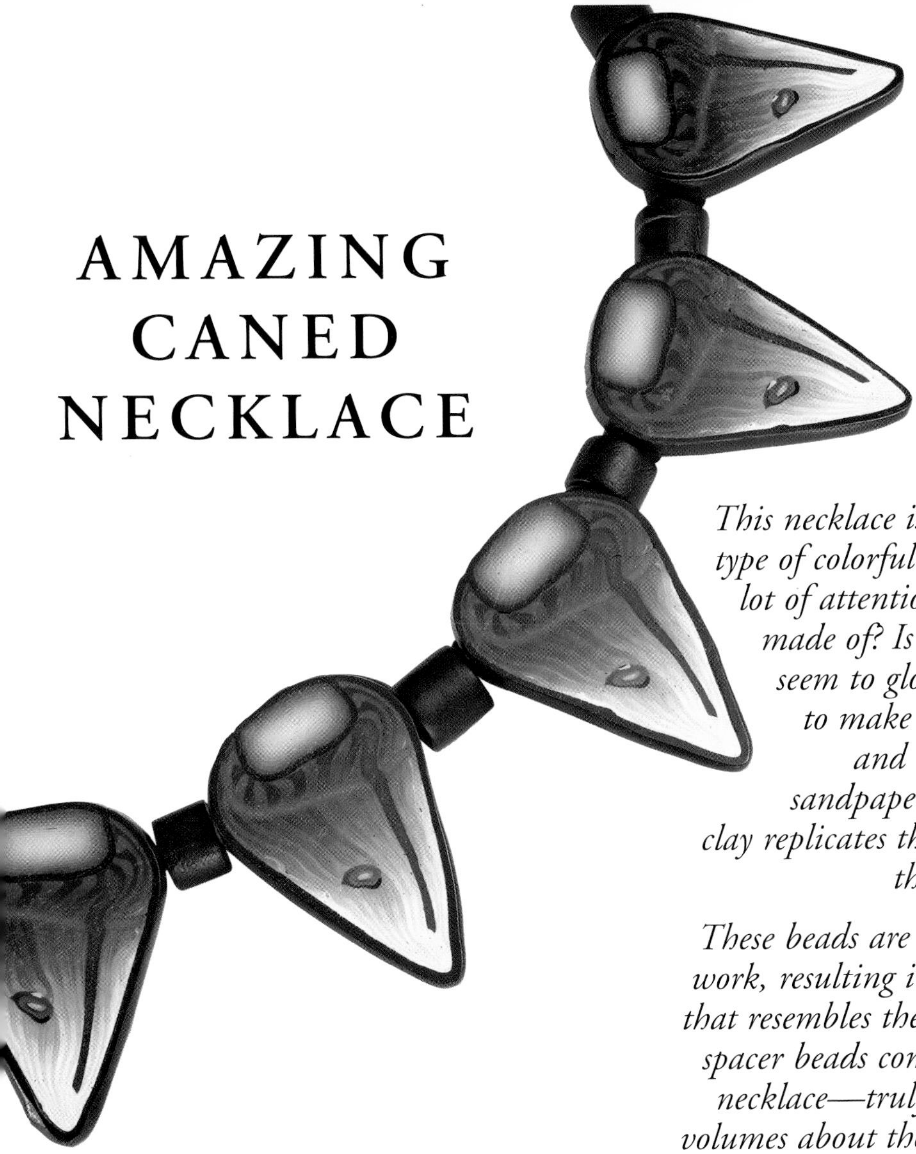

AMAZING CANED NECKLACE

This necklace is a personal favorite, because this type of colorful detail and shine always attracts a lot of attention. People are curious—what is it made of? Is it painted, and why do the colors seem to glow? Nine polyclay shades combine to make these brilliant, triangular beads, and the luster is achieved without sandpaper and buffing tools. Happily, this clay replicates the surface on which it's baked, in this case, shiny glass.

These beads are created through step-by-step cane work, resulting in a very detailed, vibrant pattern that resembles the feathers of a peacock. Handmade spacer beads complete this proud, yet inexpensive necklace—truly a unique piece that will speak volumes about the colorful personality who wears it.

Supplies:

2-ounce (56g) blocks of polymer clay: 1 each Burnt Umber, Raw Sienna, Beige, Sea Green, Ecru, Gold, Yellow, Fuchsia, Purple, Black, and Green (Premo! Sculpey)

Liquid polymer clay (Sculpey)
Tissue blade
Pasta machine
Rubber cord (Buna)
Craft glue

3" x 5" (8cm x 13cm) piece of glass
Toothpick
Bamboo skewer

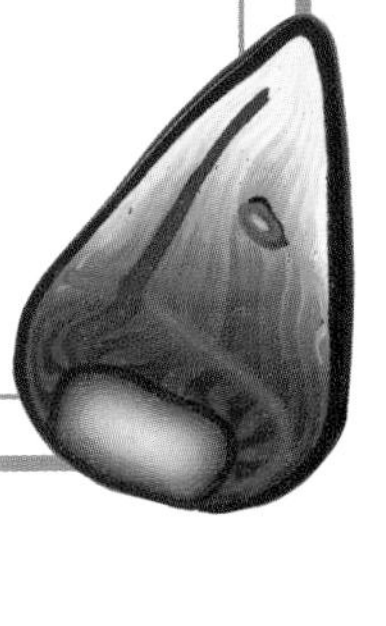

Prep: Condition clay. Roll sheets of clay on thickest setting and fold in half.

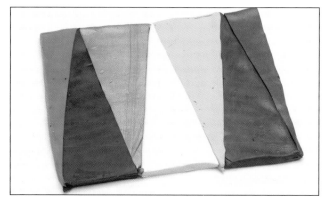

1. Cut the Green, Burnt Umber, Gold, Ecru, Beige, Raw Sienna, and Sea Green clay into triangles 1⅞" x 4⅜" (5cm x 11cm). Place triangles together as pictured. Trim ½" (1cm) off the outside two triangles. Roll this through the pasta machine on the thickest setting. Don't change the direction or fold this sheet. It should stay just as pictured above.

2. Fold the sheet in half and roll through the pasta machine 15 times on the thickest setting with the folded edge going in first. It should end up looking like step 3. Then roll this sheet through the pasta machine one more time on a medium setting.

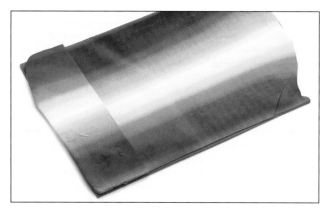

3. Cut a strip from this sheet 1½" (4 cm) wide. Flip this strip over so that the Green and Sea Green are reversed and lay it on top of the sheet. Then cut another strip the same size. Keep cutting and flipping and stacking the strips.

4. When finished cutting, flipping and stacking, cut this piece in half. Stack the two halves together with the Greens at one end and the Ecru at the other.

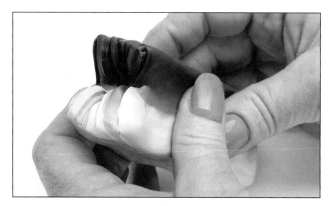

5. Compact and reduce the cane by pushing in the middle (see Reducing Cane Rods, page 9). Push on all four sides of the cane. Reduce cane so that it is about 1" high x 1¼" deep (2.5cm x 3cm). Cut off the distorted end of this cane.

6. Cut off a thin slice of the cane (see above).

7. Roll out a piece of Purple clay and form into a ball. Flatten and fit it between the sliced area.

8. Cut through the cane diagonally as pictured, from the left top corner to middle right side.

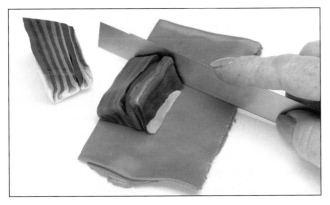

9. Roll Fuchsia clay through the pasta machine on a medium setting. Fold in half. Place a half block that was cut in step 8 on the Fuchsia sheet. Use this piece as a pattern to trim the sheet to fit the block.

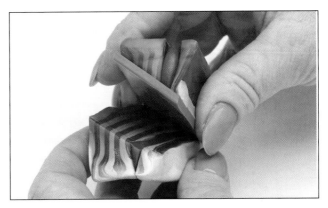

10. Put the two halves of the block back together with the Fuchsia sheet in between.

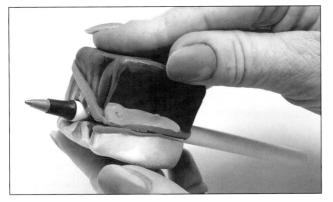

11. In order to insert a round log into this design, cut through the face of the cane on the bottom quarter of the block and press a writing pen into the clay as pictured. If the sides of the cane spread, gently push them back. You will now have a channel for the log to go in.

12. Roll a small coil of Yellow clay 1" long x ½" diameter (2.5cm x 1cm). Put a sheet of Green clay through the pasta machine on the thickest setting. Roll the sheet of Green clay around the Yellow coil. Roll the Black clay on a medium setting. Then roll the Black sheet around the Green coil.

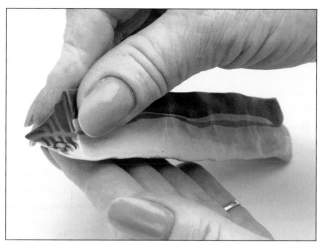

13. Place this rod into the channel made previously with the pen. Then compact the block together gently but securely. Reduce down to ¾" (2cm) square.

14. Push this into a triangle shape all the way down the length of the cane. Pinch the edges (as pictured) while pushing down in the middle to make a channel for the Purple shaded cane that you will add in the next step.

15. Make the Purple shaded cane (see making a Skinner shade page 8). Roll down the purple cane until it's ½" (1cm) in diameter. Roll Black clay through the pasta machine on a medium setting. Roll this sheet around the purple cane. Place the purple cane into the channel made previously. Roll up the pointed edges of this triangle around the purple cane.

16. Roll black clay through the pasta machine on #5 setting. Wrap this sheet round the whole cane piece except for the purple rod, which is already covered in black. Slice the rod into twenty ⅛" (0.32cm) slices.

To avoid heavy sanding and buffing, bake the slices on a sheet of glass. Press the slices firmly to glass working out the air as you go.

Bake in the oven (see baking page 9).

17. To make the black beads:

See page 31 steps 9 and 10.

Cut twenty-one each ⅞" (2cm) beads and ¼" (0.64cm) beads.

Glue the ⅞" (2cm) beads to the back of the cane slices using liquid polymer clay. Bake all beads on the glass in the oven (see page 9).

18. When the beads and slices are cool, string them on the cording alternating the ¼" (0.64cm) beads with the cane slices.

To end the necklace: Put a little glue on the end of the cording and stick it halfway into the remaining ⅞" (2cm) bead. Then glue the other end of the cording into the opposite end of the bead. Allow to dry several days.

SOURCES

Polymer clay and related supplies are widely available in craft and art materials shops. If you have problems finding these items, the following suppliers should be able to help.

The Clay Factory
P.O. Box 460598
Escondido, CA 92046
(800) 243-3466
www.clayfactoryinc.com

Shapelets, Super Slicer, Liquid Sculpey, Sculpey Glazes, Push Molds
Polyform Products
1901 Estes Ave.
Elk Grove Village, IL 60007
www.sculpey.com

Cutters
Kemper Tools, Mfg.
13595 12th St.
Chino, CA 91710
(800) 388-5367

Glue
Ultimate Glue
Crafter's Pick
520 Cleveland Ave.
Albany, CA 94710

Gold Leaf
Old World Art
1953 S. Lake Pl.
Ontario, CA 91761
www.oldworldart.com

Transfer Foils
Jones Tones
33865 United Ave.
Pueblo, CO 81001
www.jonestones.com

Piñata Inks, Pearl Ex Powders
Jacquard Products
Rupert, Gibbon & Spider, Inc.
PO Box 425
Healdsburg, CA 95448
www.jacquardproducts.com

Washi Papers
Hanko Designs
875 A Island Dr. #186
Alameda, CA 94502
(510) 523-5603
and
Yasutomo and Co.
490 Eccles Ave.
So. San Francisco, CA 94080
www.yasutomo.com

Texture Plates
Scratch Art
11 Robbie Rd.
Avon, MA 02322
www.scratchart.com

Brass Stencils
Heritage Handcrafts
P.O. Box 261176
Littleton, CO 80163
and
Stamporium
10116 50th Place West
Mukitec, WA 98275
www.stamporium.com

Rubber Stamps
ERA Graphics
1705 Big Oak Road
Placerville, CA 95667
www.ERAgraphics.com

Stylus Tip Molding Mats
Clearsnap Inc.
PO Box 98
Anacortes, WA 98221
www.clearsnap.com

Rub 'N Buff
American Art Clay
4717 W. 16th St.
Indianapolis, IN 46222
www.amaco.com

Produced by
Banar Designs, Inc.
P.O. Box 483
Fallbrook, CA 92088
www.banardesigns.com

Art Direction: Barbara Finwall
Editorial Direction: Nancy Javier
Photography: Stephen Whalen
Computer Graphics: Chris Nelsen
Project Direction: Jerilyn Clements
Writing: Susan Borsch
Editing: Jerilyn Clements, Nancy Javier
Illustrations: Victoria Dye

THE BEST *Polymer Clay Projects*
COME FROM NORTH LIGHT BOOKS!

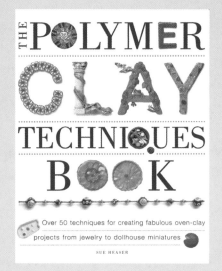

All the techniques you need to create hundreds of polymer clay projects, including buttons, beads, jewelry, figurines, boxes, mosaics and frames! Learn how to create marbling effects, simulate textures, create faux stones and more. It's all here!
ISBN 1-58180-008-8, paperback, 128 pages, #31503-K

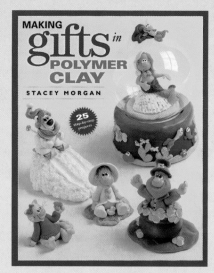

These 25 polymer clay projects are just right for beginners, both adults and children. Each one can be completed in a single sitting without a lot of fuss. Finished pieces can be used as magnets, pins, buttons or decorative figurines-perfect little gifts for friends and family alike.
ISBN 1-58180-104-1, paperback, 128 pages, #31792-K

With a little imagination, you'll learn how to bring a whole world of cheery characters to life! Full-color step-by-step photos show you how to make every detail just right, from hair to facial expressions to feet. 21 great projects in all!
ISBN 0-89134-721-6, paperback, 128 pages, #30881-K

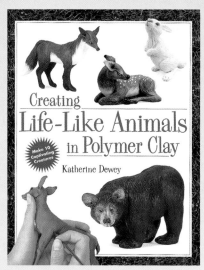

With the easy-to-use medium of polymer clay and this extraordinary book, you can learn to create exquisitely detailed animal sculptures that are full of personality. Inside you'll find step-by-step instructions for 10 charming projects, including bluebirds, white-tailed fawns, basset hounds, rabbits, bears and more. You'll even learn how to model animals to look like bronze or jade.
ISBN 0-89134-955-3, paperback, 128 pages, #31428-K

Now you can use polymer clay to create elegant designs for your home! Nineteen step-by-step projects make getting started easy. You'll learn how to combine clay with fabric, silverware and other household items, plus metallic powders that simulate colored glass, antique bronze or gleaming silver. You'll also find instructions for color mixing, marbling and caning.
ISBN 1-58180-139-4, paperback, 128 pages, #31880-K

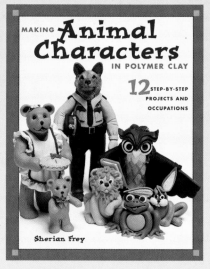

Let clay artist Sherian Frey show you how to create imaginative characters out of polymer clay. These fourteen "animal-at-work" step-by-step projects build upon technique and experience as you go. In no time you'll be shaping everything from snails, rabbits, and bears to kangaroo, dogs, and more-each one with a personality and humor all its own.
ISBN 1-58180-041-X, paperback, 128 pages, #31596-K